W9-AXK-288

SandCastle

Dollars & Cents

Let's Add
Money

Kelly Doudna

Consulting Editor Monica Marx, M.A./Reading Specialist

ABDO
Publishing Company

Published by SandCastle™, an imprint of ABDO Publishing Company, 4940 Viking Drive, Edina, Minnesota 55435.

Credits
Edited by: Pam Price
Curriculum Coordinator: Nancy Tuminelly
Cover and Interior Design and Production: Mighty Media
Photo Credits: Comstock, Eyewire Images, Hemera, PhotoDisc, Stockbyte

Library of Congress Cataloging-in-Publication Data

Doudna, Kelly, 1963-
    Let's add money / Kelly Doudna.
        p. cm. -- (Dollars & cents)
    Includes index.
    Summary: Shows how to use addition to find out whether the money two people have is enough to pay for various items and looks at different coins and bills, from a dime to a twenty-dollar bill.
    ISBN 1-57765-900-7
    1. Money--Juvenile literature. 2. Addition--Juvenile literature. [1. Money. 2. Addition.]
I. Title. II. Series.

HG221.5 .D653 2002
640'.42--dc21

                                                                        2002071182

SandCastle™ books are created by a professional team of educators, reading specialists, and content developers around five essential components that include phonemic awareness, phonics, vocabulary, text comprehension, and fluency. All books are written, reviewed, and leveled for guided reading, early intervention reading, and Accelerated Reader® programs and designed for use in shared, guided, and independent reading and writing activities to support a balanced approach to literacy instruction.

Let Us Know

After reading the book, SandCastle would like you to tell us your stories about reading. What is your favorite page? Was there something hard that you needed help with? Share the ups and downs of learning to read. We want to hear from you! To get posted on the ABDO Publishing Company Web site, send us email at:

sandcastle@abdopub.com

SandCastle Level: Transitional

Coins and bills are money.

We use coins and bills
to pay for things.

Let's see what we can buy.

$25.00

The rubber boots cost $25.00.
$25.00 = 5 five-dollar bills

Meg has 4 five-dollar bills.

Mike has 1 five-dollar bill.

Do they have enough
to buy the boots?

Let's add.
4 + 1 = 5

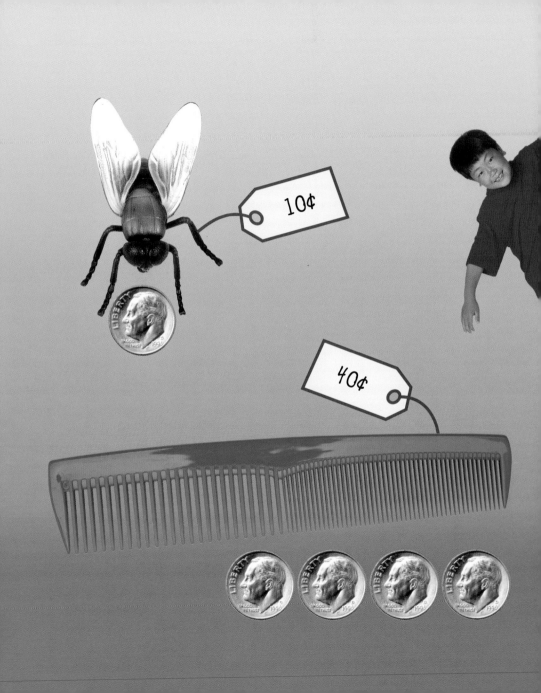

The toy fly costs 10¢.
10¢ = 1 dime

The comb costs 40¢.
40¢ = 4 dimes

How many dimes
does Ken need altogether?

Let's add.
1 + 4 = 5

$1.00

The rubber duck costs $1.00.
$1.00 = 4 quarters

Sue has 3 quarters.

Jay has 1 quarter.

Do they have enough
to buy the rubber duck?

Let's add.
3 + 1 = 4

The truck costs $1.00.
$1.00 = 1 one-dollar bill

The yo-yo costs $3.00.
$3.00 = 3 one-dollar bills

How many one-dollar bills
does Peg need altogether?

Let's add.
1 + 3 = 4

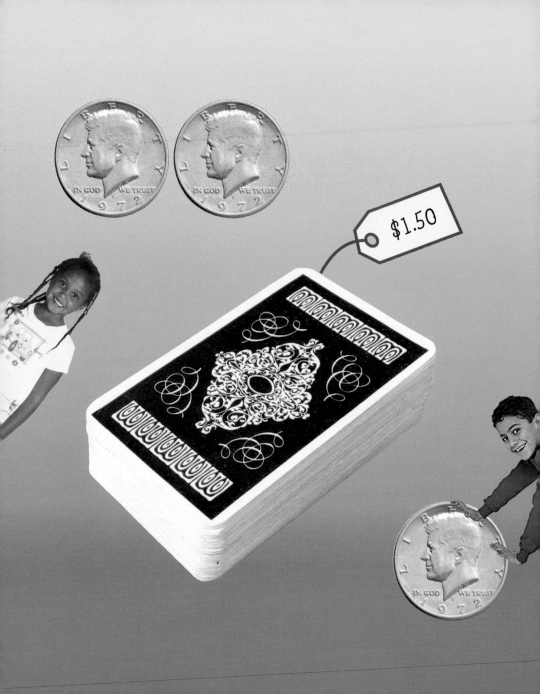

$1.50

The deck of cards costs $1.50.
$1.50 = 3 half-dollars

Brenda has 2 half-dollars.

Max has 1 half-dollar.

Do they have enough
to buy the cards?

Let's add.
2 + 1 = 3

The rocket costs $10.00.
$10.00 = 1 ten-dollar bill

The globe costs $20.00.
$20.00 = 2 ten-dollar bills

How many ten-dollar bills
does Tom need altogether?

Let's add.
1 + 2 = 3

The baseball glove costs $40.00.
$40.00 = 2 twenty-dollar bills

Lisa has 1 twenty-dollar bill.

Sam has 1 twenty-dollar bill.

Do they have enough
to buy the glove?

Let's add.
$1 + 1 = 2$

What are these coins and bills called?

How much are they worth?

one dime = 10¢
one quarter = 25¢
one half-dollar = 50¢
one dollar = $1.00
five dollars = $5.00
ten dollars = $10.00
twenty dollars = $20.00

Index

Glossary

boots   heavy footwear designed to protect the feet and ankles

comb   an instrument with teeth used to groom hair

glove   a covering designed to protect the hand

rocket   a powerful engine often used to propel space vehicles

yo-yo   a disk with a groove in the middle that travels up and down a string

About SandCastle™

A professional team of educators, reading specialists, and content developers created the SandCastle™ series to support young readers as they develop reading skills and strategies and increase their general knowledge. The SandCastle™ series has four levels that correspond to early literacy development in young children. The levels are provided to help teachers and parents select the appropriate books for young readers.

Emerging Readers
(no flags)

Beginning Readers
(1 flag)

Transitional Readers
(2 flags)

Fluent Readers
(3 flags)

These levels are meant only as a guide. All levels are subject to change.

ABDO
Publishing Company

To see a complete list of SandCastle™ books and other nonfiction titles from ABDO Publishing Company, visit www.abdopub.com or contact us at:

4940 Viking Drive, Edina, Minnesota 55435 • 1-800-800-1312 • fax: 1-952-831-1632